HAL•LEONARD

ro vocal®
BETTER THAN KARAOKE!

NGBOOK & SOUND-ALIKE CD
TH UNIQUE *PITCH-CHANGER*™

WOMEN'S EDITION
VOLUME 17

Jazz Ballads

T0081547

ISBN 978-1-4234-2151-1

HAL•LEONARD®
CORPORATION

7777 W. BLUEMOUND RD. P.O. BOX 13819 MILWAUKEE, WI 53213

Visit Hal Leonard Online at
www.halleonard.com

CONTENTS

Body and Soul

Words by Edward Heyman, Robert Sour and Frank Eyton
Music by John Green

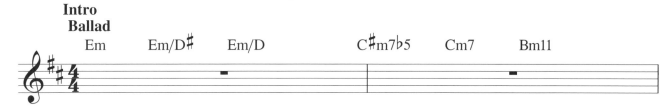

Intro
Ballad

Em   Em/D#   Em/D   C#m7b5   Cm7   Bm11

G#m7b5 A/G F#m11 G/F Csus2/E Ebmaj7b5 G/D C#m7b5 C9#11   B7#5

Verse

Em   B7b9   Em⁶⁄₉   A7#5

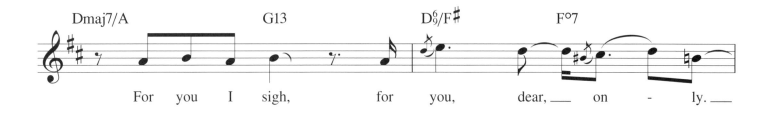

1. My ___ heart is ___ sad   and lone - ly.

Dmaj7/A   G13   D⁶⁄₉/F#   F°7

For you I sigh,   for you, dear, ___ on - ly. ___

Em7   Gmaj7/D   C#m11   F#7#5

___   Why ___ have - n't you   seen ___ it? ___

Gmaj7 E7/G# A9sus4   Dmaj9 G9 F#m7b5 B13

I'm all for you, ___ bod - y and soul.

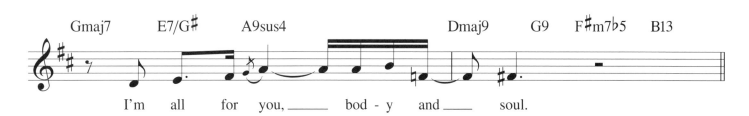

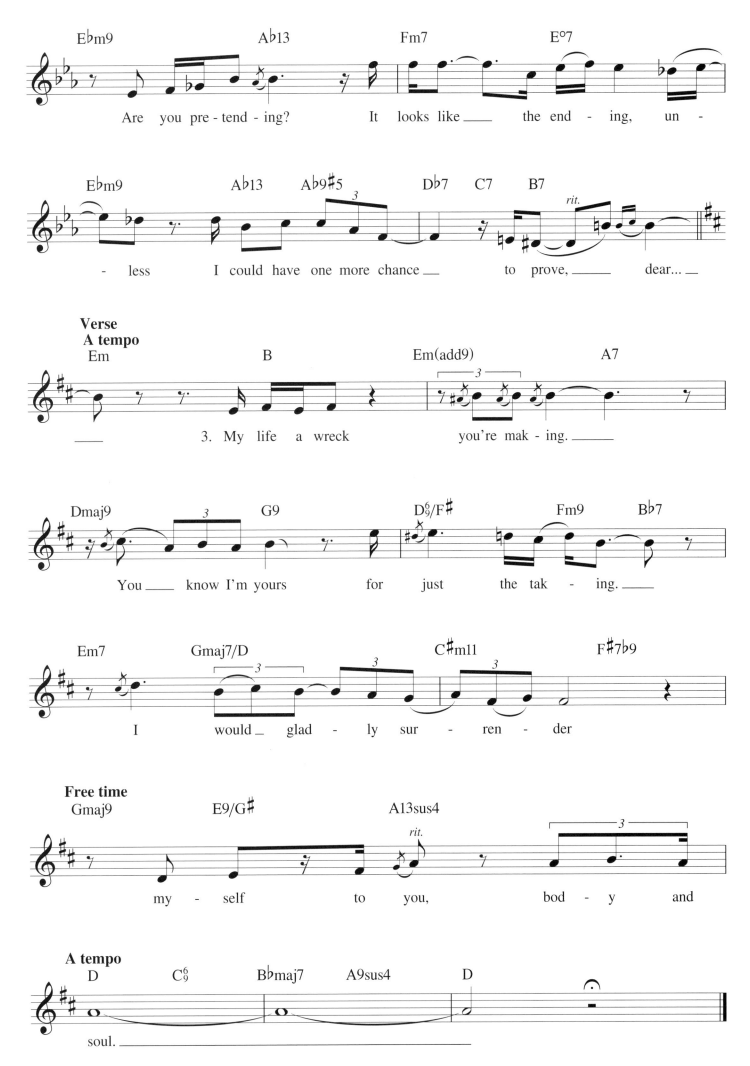

A Child Is Born

Music by Thad Jones
Lyrics by Alec Wilder

Intro
Slowly

Bb   Ebm6/9   Bb   Ebm6/9

Verse

Bbmaj7   Ebm6/9   Bbmaj7

1. Now ____ out of ____ the ____ night, ____

Ebm6   Bbmaj9   Ebm6

new as ____ the dawn, ____ in - to ____ the

Am7b5   D7#9   Gm(add9)

light. This child,

D7b9#5   Gm(add9)   D7#9#5

in - no - cent ____ child, ____ soft as ____ a

Gm9   C9   F13sus4

fawn, this child is born. ____

Verse

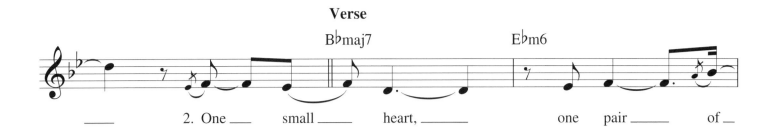

_____ 2. One _____ small _____ heart, _____ one pair of _____

_____ eyes, _____ one work _____ of art _____

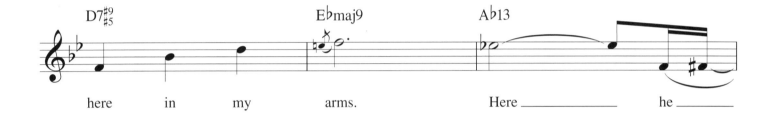

here in my arms. Here _____ he _____

_____ lies, _____ trust - ing _____ and _____ warm. _____

Bless - ed this morn, _____ a child _____ is

A tempo

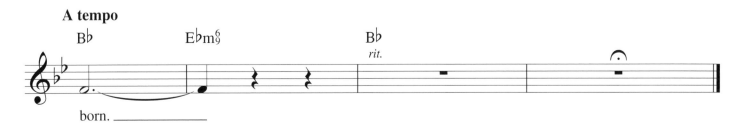

born. _____

For All We Know

Words by Sam M. Lewis
Music by J. Fred Coots

C#°7 ... Cm11

night _____ un - til _____ the last min - ute. ___

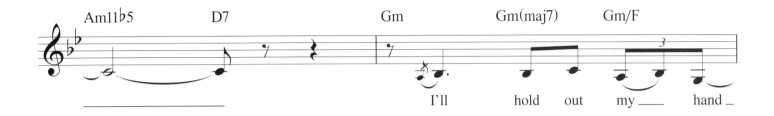

Am11♭5   D7   Gm   Gm(maj7)   Gm/F

_____ I'll hold out my ____ hand ___

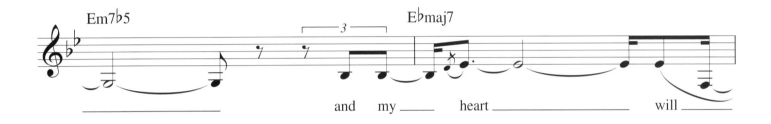

Em7♭5   E♭maj7

_____ and my ____ heart _____ will ____

Verse

Cm9   F7   F13♭9   B♭maj7

____ be in ____ it. _____ 2. For all _____ we ___

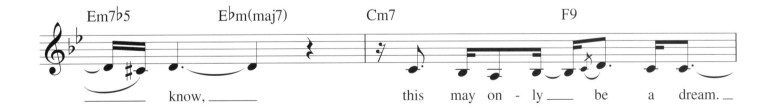

Em7♭5   E♭m(maj7)   Cm7   F9

_____ know, _____ this may on - ly ____ be a dream. ___

Cm7   F13   B♭maj9

____ We ____ come _____ and ___

go _____ like __ a rip-ple in a stream. _____

_____ So love me to -

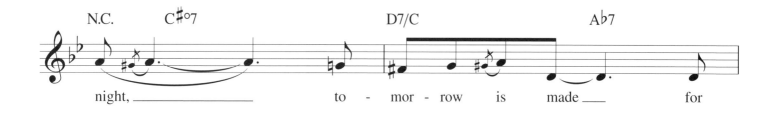

night, _____ to - mor - row is made ___ for

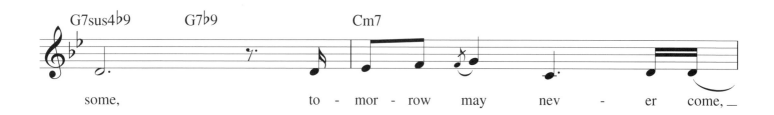

some, to - mor - row may nev - er come, __

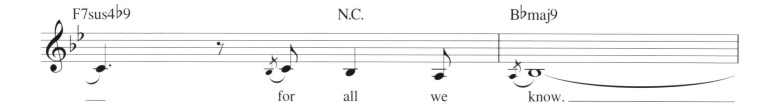

___ for all we know. _____

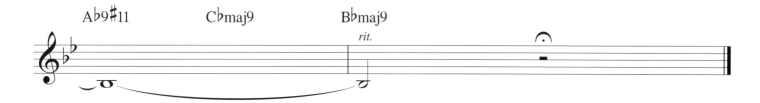

_____

My Foolish Heart

from MY FOOLISH HEART
Words by Ned Washington
Music by Victor Young

fas - ci - na - tion _____ or _____ a dream __ that will fade _____ and __

fall a - part, it's _____ love, _____ this time it's

Outro

love, my fool - ish heart. _____

It's

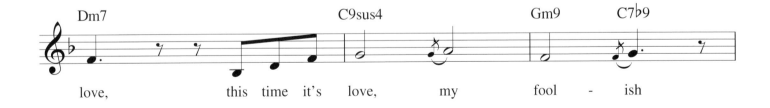

love, this time it's love, my fool - ish

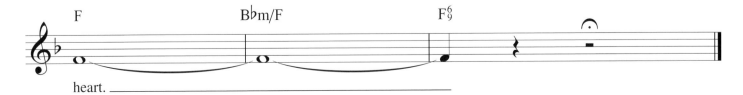

heart. _____

Lover Man
(Oh, Where Can You Be?)

By Jimmy Davis, Roger Ramirez and Jimmy Sherman

Verse

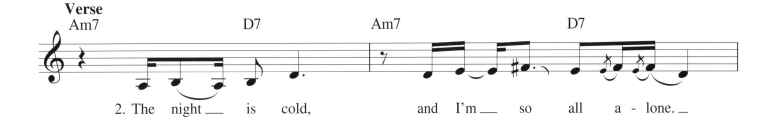

2. The night __ is cold, and I'm __ so all a - lone. __

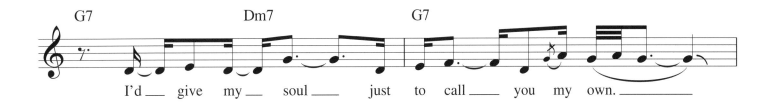

I'd __ give my __ soul __ just to call __ you my own. __

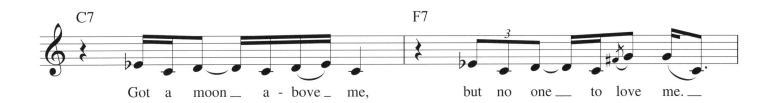

Got a moon __ a - bove _ me, but no one __ to love me. __

Lov - er man, __ oh, where __ can you be? __

Bridge

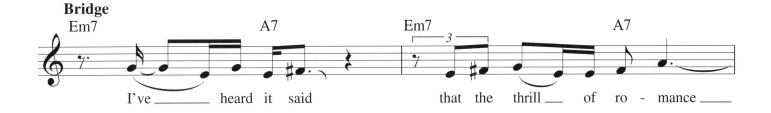

I've ___ heard it said that the thrill __ of ro - mance __

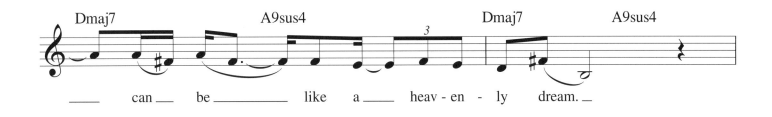

___ can __ be ___ like a __ heav - en - ly dream. __

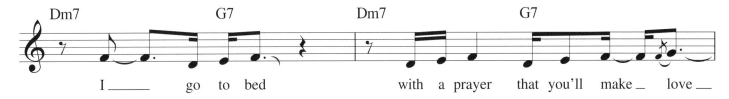

I ___ go to bed with a prayer that you'll make __ love

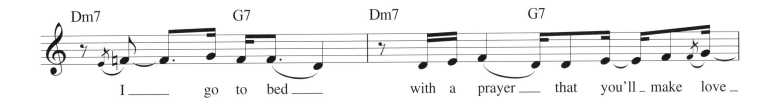

I ____ go to bed ____ with a prayer ___ that you'll _ make love _

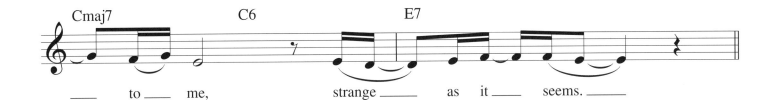

____ to ___ me, strange ____ as it ___ seems. ____

Verse

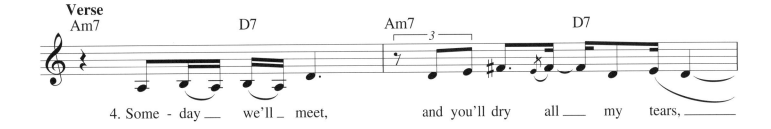

4. Some - day ___ we'll _ meet, and you'll dry all ___ my tears, ____

___ then ___ whis - per ___ sweet lit - tle things in my ears, ____

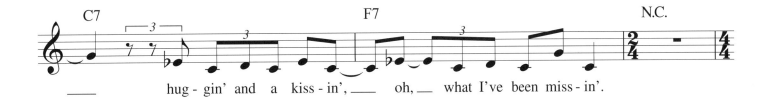

____ hug - gin' and a kiss - in', ____ oh, ___ what I've been miss - in'.

Slower

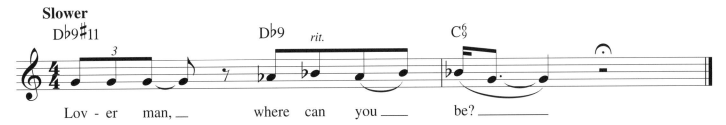

Lov - er man, ___ where can you ____ be? ____

The Nearness of You

from the Paramount Picture ROMANCE IN THE DARK
Words by Ned Washington
Music by Hoagy Carmichael

Night Song

from GOLDEN BOY
Lyric by Lee Adams
Music by Charles Strouse

Bridge

Fm7   B♭9sus4   B♭9

Where do you go _____ when you feel that

E♭6/9   Am9

your brain is on fire? _____ Where do you go when

D9sus4   D9   Gmaj7

you don't e - ven know what it is you de - sire? _____

Esus4

Lis - ten,   laugh - ter ev - 'ry - where,

hear it,   life is in the

E   Dm7   G7♯5   **Verse** C6/9

air.   3. As the _____ night _____ comes, __

_____ and the town _____ a - wakes,   sound of chil -

26

Unforgettable

Words and Music by Irving Gordon

love that clings to me, oh, how the thought of you does things to me. Nev-er be-fore has some-one been more.

Verse

2. Un - for - get - ta - ble, ooh, in ev - 'ry way, and for - ev - er more, that's how you'll stay.

Pro Vocal® Series

SONGBOOK & SOUND-ALIKE CD
SING 8 GREAT SONGS
WITH A PROFESSIONAL BAND

Whether you're a karaoke singer or an auditioning professional, the Pro Vocal® series is for you! Unlike most karaoke packs, each book in the Pro Vocal Series contains the lyrics, melody, and chord symbols for eight hit songs. The CD contains demos for listening, and separate backing tracks so you can sing along. The CD is playable on any CD player, but it is also enhanced so PC and Mac computer users can adjust the recording to any pitch without changing the tempo! Perfect for home rehearsal, parties, auditions, corporate events, and gigs without a backup band.

MIXED EDITIONS

These editions feature songs for both male and female voices.

FOR MORE INFORMATION, SEE YOUR LOCAL MUSIC DEALER, OR WRITE TO:

HAL•LEONARD®
CORPORATION
7777 W. BLUEMOUND RD. P.O. BOX 13819 MILWAUKEE, WI 53213

Visit Hal Leonard online at www.halleonard.com

Prices, contents, & availability subject to change without notice.
Disney charaters and artwork © Disney Enterprises, Inc.

0909

ORIGINAL KEYS FOR SINGERS

ACROSS THE UNIVERSE

Authentic vocal/piano transcriptions of 20 Beatles tunes from the Golden Globe and Oscar-nominated musical directed by Julie Taymor. Includes: Because • Blackbird • Hey Jude • Let It Be • Revolution • Something • and more.
00307010 Vocal Transcriptions with Piano $19.95

MARIAH CAREY

Vocal transcriptions of all five octaves of this pop diva's 20 most popular tunes, including: Always Be My Baby • Dreamlover • Emotions • Heartbreaker • Hero • I Don't Wanna Cry • Love Takes Time • Loverboy • One Sweet Day • Vision of Love • We Belong Together • and more.
00306835 Vocal Transcriptions with Piano $19.95

PATSY CLINE

The definitive Patsy Cline book for singers! 27 top songs in the original key, newly transcribed from the original recordings. For voice with piano accompaniment, with chord symbols. Includes: Always • Blue Moon of Kentucky • Crazy • Faded Love • I Fall to Pieces • Just a Closer Walk with Thee • Sweet Dreams • more. Also includes a biography.
00740072 Vocal Transcriptions with Piano $14.95

ELLA FITZGERALD

This fine book features authentic transcriptions in the original keys of 25 Fitzgerald classics in voice with piano accompaniment format: A-tisket, A-tasket • But Not for Me • Easy to Love • Embraceable You • The Lady Is a Tramp • Misty • Oh, Lady Be Good! • Satin Doll • Stompin' at the Savoy • Take the "A" Train • and more. Includes a biography and discography.
00740252 Vocal Transcriptions with Piano $16.95

JOSH GROBAN

Alejate • Awake • Believe • February Song • In Her Eyes • L'Ultima Notte • Lullaby • Machine • Mai • Never Let Go • Now or Never • O Holy Night • Per Te • The Prayer • Remember When It Rained • So She Dances • To Where You Are • Un Amore Per Sempre • Un Dia Llegara • You Are Loved (Don't Give Up) • You Raise Me Up • You're Still You.
00306969 Vocal Transcriptions with Piano $19.99

BILLIE HOLIDAY

Transcribed from Historic Recordings

This groundbreaking publication features authentic transcriptions in the original keys of 19 classics from the key signature recordings of the great Lady Day. Includes a biography and discography, and these standards in voice with piano accompaniment format: All of Me • Billie's Blues (I Love My Man) • Body and Soul • Crazy He Calls Me • Easy Living • Fine and Mellow • A Fine Romance • God Bless' the Child • Good Morning Heartache • I Cried for You • I Wished on the Moon • Lover, Come Back to Me • Miss Brown to You • Solitude • Some Other Spring • Strange Fruit • This Year's Kisses • The Very Thought of You • You've Changed.
00740140 Vocal Transcriptions with Piano $14.95

DIANA KRALL

20 of the signature songs of jazz vocalist/pianist Diana Krall. Includes: All or Nothing at All • The Frim Fram Sauce • The Girl in the Other Room • Hit That Jive Jack • The Look of Love • 'S Wonderful • This Can't Be Love • and more.
00306743 Vocal Transcriptions with Piano $19.95

NANCY LAMOTT

Cabaret singer Nancy LaMott died in 1995 at age 43, leaving behind five CDs filled with her signature songs arranged and played by her music director, Christopher Marlowe. 21 of these beloved renditions are available here: Autumn Leaves • Downtown • I Have Dreamed • It Might as Well Be Spring • Moon River • Skylark • That Old Black Magic • and more.
00306995 Vocal Transcriptions with Piano $19.99

THE BEST OF LIZA MINNELLI

25 signature standards, all transcribed exactly as recorded, in their original keys! Includes: And All That Jazz • Cabaret • Losing My Mind • Maybe This Time • Me and My Baby • Theme from "New York, New York" • Ring Them Bells • Sara Lee • Say Liza (Liza with a Z) • Shine It On • Sing Happy • The Singer • Taking a Chance on Love.
00306928 Vocal Transcriptions with Piano $19.99

THE VERY BEST OF FRANK SINATRA

40 swingin' Sinatra classic tunes arranged in their original keys. Includes: Come Fly with Me • I've Got You Under My Skin • It Was a Very Good Year • My Way • Night and Day • Summer Wind • The Way You Look Tonight • You Make Me Feel So Young • and more. Includes biography.
00306753 Vocal Transcriptions with Piano $19.95

STEVE TYRELL – BACK TO BACHARACH

Our matching folio to Steve Tyrell's tribute to Burt Bacharach features the actual vocal transcriptions of 14 classics, including: Alfie • Always Something There to Remind Me • Close to You • I Say a Little Prayer • The Look of Love • Raindrops Keep Fallin' on My Head • This Guy's in Love with You • Walk on By • and more.
00307024 Vocal Transcriptions with Piano $16.99

SARAH VAUGHAN

The *All Music Guide* calls Vaughan "one of the most wondrous voices of the 20th century." This collection gathers 25 of her classics arranged in her original keys so today's singers can try to match her performances. Songs include: Black Coffee • But Not for Me • Cherokee (Indian Love Song) • Darn That Dream • East of the Sun (And West of the Moon) • If You Could See Me Now • It Might as Well Be Spring • Lullaby of Birdland • The Man I Love • My Funny Valentine • The Nearness of You • A Night in Tunisia • Perdido • September Song • Tenderly • and more.
00306558 Vocal Transcriptions with Piano $17.95

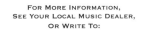